COLONIAL
Germantown
MENNONITES

COLONIAL
Germantown
MENNONITES

Leonard Gross and Jan Gleysteen

Leonard Gross *Jan Gleysteen*

Foreword by
John L. Ruth

Cascadia
Publishing House
Telford, Pennsylvania

copublished with
Herald Press
Scottdale, Pennsylvania

Cascadia Publishing House orders, information, reprint permissions:
contact@CascadiaPublishingHouse.com
1-215-723-9125
126 Klingerman Road, Telford PA 18969
www.CascadiaPublishingHouse.com

Colonial Germantown Mennonites
Copyright © 2007 by Cascadia Publishing House, Telford, PA 18969
All rights reserved
Copublished with Herald Press, Scottdale, PA
Library of Congress Catalog Number: 2006026347
ISBN 10: 1-931038-41-4; *ISBN 13:* 978-1-931038-41-6
Book design by Cascadia Publishing House
Cover design by Gwen M. Stamm

The paper used in this publication is recycled and meets the
minimum requirements of American National Standard for Information
Sciences—Permanence of Paper for Printed Library Materials,
ANSI Z39.48-1984.1984

Grateful acknowledgment is made for permission
to use materials listed in the "Photo Credits" section, p. 79

Cover illustration: courtesy, Germantown Mennonite Historic Trust:
A lithograph by Grant Simon, 1955, titled *Mennonite Meeting, 1770.*

Library of Congress Cataloguing-in-Publication Data
Gross, Leonard, 1931 Nov. 17-
Colonial Germantown Mennonites / Leonard Gross and Jan Gleysteen ; fore-
word by John L. Ruth.
     p. cm.
Includes bibliographical references.
  ISBN-13: 978-1-931038-41-6 (5.5 x 8.5" trade pbk. : alk. paper)
  ISBN-10: 1-931038-41-4 (5.5 x 8.5" trade pbk. : alk. paper)
1. Germantown (Philadelphia, Pa.)--History. 2. Historic buildings--Pennsylva-
nia--Philadelphia. 3. Historic sites--Pennsylvania--Philadelphia. 4. Mennonites--
Pennsylvania--Philadelphia--History. 5. Mennonites--Pennsylvania--Philadelphia-
-Social life and customs. 6. Germantown (Philadelphia, Pa.)--Buildings, struc-
tures, etc. 7. Philadelphia (Pa.)--Buildings, structures, etc. 8. Philadelphia (Pa.)--
History--Colonial period, ca. 1600-1775. 9. Germantown (Philadelphia, Pa.)--
Tours. 10. Philadelphia (Pa.)--Tours. I. Gleysteen, Jan. II. Title.

F159.G3G76 2007
974.8'1102--dc22

                                                                          2006026347

15 14 13 12 11 10 09 08 07 06   10 9 8 7 6 5 4 3 2 1

"A Cloud of Witnesses"

To those worthy and faithful
Germantown witnesses who have gone on before us:

Walter Temple
Eleanor Temple
Stanley Fretz
Horace Kratz
Melvin and Verna Gingerich
Roman Stutzman
Robert F. Ulle

To two worthy and faithful
ermantown witnesses who have stayed the course
these past three and more decades:

Ruth Fireoved Marino
Marianna (Mrs. Roman) Stutzman

Contents

The Concord Schoolhouse
The Upper Burial Ground
Father Kelpius' Cave
The Brethren Meetinghouse
Christopher Sauer's Print Shop

Foreword

"**I** NEVER SAW MORE SIMPLICITY," recorded the famous evangelist George Whitefield in 1740, after preaching at Skippack in southeastern Pennsylvania. Had he ridden fifteen miles back through the woods to Germantown, and viewed the Mennonite meetinghouse there, he would doubtless have mused further. For even the successor of that log building of 1708, built of stone in 1770, greets a twenty-first century eye as a statement of simplicity.

More than that, as this guidebook explains, Germantown's Mennonite meetinghouse is an expression of continuity. It was children and grandchildren of European Mennonites who gathered here along the town's only major street, in the first of their people's congregations to endure in America. The location was the site of a homestead bought by a Dutch-speaking paper-maker four years after the town's founding in 1683.

Willem Rittinghuysen (William Rittenhouse) had immigrated from Amsterdam with his wife Gertruid and three children. The first paper-maker in the English colonies, he was also elected in 1698 as its first Mennonite minister. By then he and his partner-son Nicholas had already moved out of town to the site of their mill along the nearby Wissahickon Creek. It was in

his Lower Rhenish accent, in the house of Mennonite neighbor
Isaac van Bebber, that the slowly accruing congregation heard
the scriptural message for a decade.

Willem himself never saw the log meetinghouse built in the
months following his unexpected death in 1708. Nor will we
see it. What we can visit is the sturdy stone replacement that
served the congregation for two centuries after 1770. "Simple,
substantial and beautiful," to use the phrase of a Lancaster
County Mennonite preacher, it has become an icon of American Mennonite memory, even while its surroundings have
changed beyond the imagination of its first users.

Location can speak. Standing in the doorway and looking
outward, one faces, across the urban horizon, in the direction of
the paper mill site on a branch of the Wissahickon Creek. A tiny
village of buildings there, one bearing the date of 1707, evokes
physically—unlike the written-only records of earlier and temporary Mennonite dwellings in Manhattan or along the
Delaware Bay—the earliest permanent Mennonite dwelling
outside of Europe. The quiet stream running through the dell
still called Rittenhousetown reminds us of the mill it once pow-
ered. And back in the heart of the main town, the north-south
angle of Germantown Avenue recalls the Indian trail along
which a lot fell to the community's first Mennonite couple, Jan
and Mercken Lensen, at the town's very beginning in the late
fall of 1683.

The earliest stones clustered next to the meetinghouse do
not reach far enough back to include Jan and Mercken's names.
But names such as Cassel, Funk, Keyser, and Rittenhouse de-
clare that this Mennonite community was a convergence. The
hearts that beat here came from at least four different regions of
Europe, both urban and rural. Some names are Palatine, sug-
gesting spiritual origins in Zurich, while others witness to the
heritage of Menno Simons of Friesland. This realization flavors
our recognition of the varieties of the present residents of this
historic community. It also reminds us that the church of

Christ will always be about bringing together a family that transcends nations, cultures and languages. History is here in layers. Native Americans visited in the first huts; schoolmaster Christopher Dock held summer schools here; peach trees once picturesquely lined the street running by Dirk Keyser's gracious residence; George Washington's troops met in confused shock with British redcoats in front of the Meetinghouse; a congregation struggled for two centuries after most of their people had moved into the country. It was after 1960 when a flock surprisingly regathered from many points to worship in this modern urban setting with a long memory.

The miraculously enduring meetinghouse along Germantown Avenue has become a place to meditate on how spiritual concerns leave their testimony. Those miscellaneous Mennonites living in a straggling village three centuries ago had come from a variety of motives—including persecution and economic opportunity. But in this rustic village of linen-weavers they brought to common focus what they believed. Instead of merging their identities in a generic spirituality, they insisted on being responsible to their parental church fellowships in Europe. Even before electing a preacher, "they tried to instruct each other," meeting in homes. They waited twenty-five years to celebrate a communion which they believed was an accountable one. Then they chose leaders from all four of the main communities of their European backgrounds. And built a meetinghouse. In that remarkable, scrupulous convergence, they became the departing point, and an example, for a fellowship that would spread across North America.

May this careful guidebook, in both word and image, instruct our imagination, helping us to be intelligent and appreciative pilgrims as we come back to visit Germantown.

—*John L. Ruth*
Harleysville, Pennsylvania

Authors' Preface

WHO ARE THE MENNONITES? Mennonite roots, historically, go back almost five centuries to the era of the Protestant Reformation in Europe. The beginning point of this Reformation is often considered to be the year 1517, when, it is said, Martin Luther nailed his Ninety-Five Theses to the door of the Wittenberg Castle Church that eventful day of October 31. Unrest, renewal, and protest—sometimes actual revolt—were part and parcel of these social and religious stirrings.

Ulrich Zwingli soon followed in Zurich, Switzerland, where in 1519 he attempted renewal by preaching directly to the people from the Bible, in their own language. This abrupt change in worship patterns also signaled new hopes for spiritual revival, based on the way of Jesus in the Gospels.

By 1525, some of Zwingli's followers were convinced something was amiss where the state took on the authority to control the church. These followers, wanting to remain true to the primary authority of Christ as Lord, decided to disobey the state to remain obedient to Christ. This movement came to be called Anabaptism, the birth date of which was January 21, 1525.

On that Saturday evening, a small group broke away from the Zurich state church and baptized one another at the home of Felix Mantz. The original core of believers was of one mind about the nature of the body of Christ: It was based, they believed, on a conscious gathering together of those who personally wanted to follow Christ, whom they saw as the Prince of Peace. Such following entailed attempting to witness to and live out a life of love and reconciliation with one another, and indeed, with everyone in this world. This way of reconciliation included accepting suffering as Jesus had done rather than to respond in retaliation. Known as the Swiss Brethren, they attempted also to meet the spiritual and physical needs of one another, mutually, and to reach out to others in need.

The Anabaptist movement spread. By 1530 and in years after, it had reached the northeast corner of what is today France, continuing into the Low Countries and northern Germany. Although many Anabaptists continued to affirm Christ's gospel of peace as their understanding of Christianity, a few turned revolutionary. In 1534-35, these revolutionaries legally gained control of the German city of Münster, where they then used physical force in trying to defend their city.

Out of this chaos, in 1536, Menno Simons arose as leader able to bring most of the Low Country Anabaptists—spread from what are today Belgium and the Netherlands, all the way to Poland—onto the foundation of the way of peace and love. The movement in these geographic areas soon would become known as "Mennonite."

A third group of Anabaptists originated in Austria and in what is today the Czech Republic, in 1528. They came to be known as "Hutterites," a close-knit group that holds to the idea of community of goods. In the 1870s they immigrated to North America. Today the Hutterites may be found in most of the states and provinces from Minnesota and Manitoba on westward. The Amish, who originated in a split within the Swiss Brethren in 1693, are also found in North America.

Today, in North America, apart from the Hutterites and the Amish as well as several Brethren denominations, most

Anabaptist groups, including those with direct roots in Switzer-land, go by the name *Mennonite.*

WHAT IS THE GERMANTOWN MENNONITE HISTORIC TRUST?
The Germantown Mennonite Historic Trust (before 1994 named the Germantown Mennonite Church Corporation) came into being in 1952 and reorganized in 1970. The purpose of that trust was and is to safeguard and preserve the German-town Mennonite Meetinghouse, built in 1770. The Trust is a legal corporation, entrusted with the ownership of the Meeting-house for the purpose of maintaining the structure and promot-ing its history.

GERMANTOWN'S UNIQUE SIGNIFICANCE Germantown has been called, rightfully, "the Mennonite gateway into North America." It is the Brethren gateway as well. And most certainly, it is also the German gateway—and so celebrated by Germany at the time of Germantown's Tercentenary in 1983 (see the commemorative stamp issued on the occasion, below, p. 34). With passion, Mennonite historian Robert Kreider, engaging a prepublication draft of this book, noted "the unique signifi-cance of Germantown in the experience of North American Mennonites and Brethren."

Germantown thus holds a rich history for the Mennonites and likeminded peace churches—as well as many others—in-terested in Colonial America and the variety of ideas and expe-riences that existed there, three and more centuries ago. Roots play an important part in determining who we are. And the na-ture of the roots, at their deepest level, affects us even three and more centuries later—whether we are aware of this or not.

We hope the reader will connect the story with the actual sites presently in Germantown. And we hope they will in doing so discover matters of meaningful substance and spirit.

—*Leonard Gross and Jan Gleysteen*
 Goshen, Indiana

Acknowledgments

OUR SINCERE THANKS GO TO THESE SUPPORTERS, who have contributed to the development of this volume at its various stages by providing significant corrections, suggestions, and/or additions which were then incorporated into the finalized text:

John Arn	Donald Durnbaugh
Ray Hacker	Ruth Fireoved Marino
Stephen Marino	Marcus Miller
John F. Murray	Randy Nyce
John L. Ruth	David Rempel Smucker
Keith Sprunger	Gwen Stamm
Lamont Woelk	

SUPPORTERS WHO HAVE CONTRIBUTED FINANCIALLY to this publication in a major way:

Stephen and Ruth (Fireoved) Marino
Henry and Charlotte Rosenberger
Ellen Jacobs Herr
Philip Weber

MEMBERS OF THE BOARD of the Germantown Mennonite Historic Trust

SUPPORTERS WHO TRANSFORMED A MANUSCRIPT, photos, line drawings, captions, and a map into a published volume: Michael A. King and his Cascadia Publishing House associates.

I

Historical Background

HOW DID GERMANTOWN BEGIN? The name *Pennsylvania*, during its first century of existence, conjures up memories of many "peaceable" Colonial stories, going back to 1682 when the Quaker William Penn established Philadelphia, the City of Brotherly Love. Already eight years previous, in 1674, William Penn had been a trustee for Edward Billing, a bankrupt Quaker. At that time, Penn was involved in buying and then settling New Jersey colonies, with constitutions that included religious toleration and civil rights, based on a democratic form of government.

In 1681 Penn obtained from the Crown, Charles II, in payment for a debt owed to his father, a grant of vast and rich lands to the west of the Delaware River. The king christened it "Penn Sylvania" (Penn's Woods) over the vigorous objections of the modest Quaker. In 1682 William Penn organized this new territory, proclaiming equal legal rights for the Delaware Indians and toleration for persecuted Quakers and Mennonites—as well as many others who would later arrive, such as the Brethren and Moravians.

Here was a veritable "Holy Experiment" with a vision of a society where all would get along with one another in peace and tranquility. As part of this experiment in peace, Penn in 1683 invited a number of Dutch and German artisans, including the Mennonites (and a few years later, the Brethren and the Moravians), to come to Pennsylvania. They would put down roots some seven miles northwest of the Philadelphia harbor in a brand new settlement called German Town—since 1854, an integral part of the city of Philadelphia.

PEACE-CHURCH COMMONALITIES. Brethren (Church of the Brethren), Mennonites, and Quakers (the Society of Friends) hold in common a historical witness against war. Their rubbing shoulders in Germantown in the 1680s and thereafter (the Church of the Brethren, after 1719) mutually strengthened this peace testimony. The Quakers probably influenced the other two groups in matters of attire, the simplicity of their meetinghouses, and church governance.

These historic peace churches opposed violence in North America from the outset, including in their relations with Native Americans. Respect for Indians, based on fairness and a discerning program of material aid, proved largely successful over the years. During the Revolutionary War these same peace-church groups opposed the violence and rebellion at hand and proclaimed their desire to be exempt from military duty.

MENNONITES IN AMERICA, BEFORE GERMANTOWN. Before 1683, there had been previous attempts by Mennonites to colonize on American soil, but they did not bear fruit. The trading post New Amsterdam on the Hudson (today, New York City) counted a number of Dutch Mennonites among its citizens, but we have no record of an established congregation nor of a continued Mennonite presence.

In 1659 Pieter Cornelisz Plockhoy of Zierikzee, Holland, proposed an ideal Christian Society to be established in the New Netherlands (present-day Delaware). Four years later, on July 28, 1663, the ship *Sint Jacob* dropped off forty-one persons, their farm implements and personal goods, on the banks of the Horekill, at a place they called "Swaenendael" (Valley of Swans). Apparently Plockhoy himself was not among these first settlers.

The Plockhoy settlement was based on a fundamental constitution which, among other things, prohibited slavery. This Mennonite document is the earliest known instance of a group's establishing its formal opposition to slavery in what would evolve as the Thirteen Colonies.

Unfortunately, their Christian experiment was short-lived. Within a year the British navy, ordered to destroy all non-English settlements along the Atlantic coast, leveled Plockhoy's colony "down to a very naile." More than thirty years later, an aged married couple wandered into Germantown—Plockhoy's blind son, with his wife! They spent their final years among Mennonites who, in the meantime, had become more successful in planting a community in North America.

A SPECIAL SHIP, THE CONCORD. When Penn received the province in the New World from King Charles II, he and his aides actively promoted the virgin province as a new home for interested Quakers, Mennonites, and Pietists in Holland, Germany, Switzerland, and Great Britain. On June 18, 1683, eleven families and two single men from the Krefeld area embarked at Rotterdam for London, where a Quaker merchant had booked passage for them on the *Concord*. Some of these were Mennonite; some Mennonites who had taken on the Quaker faith; and one or more possibly Quaker converts from the Reformed tradition.

The *Concord* reached the one-year-old city of Philadelphia on October 6, 1683. From there the new arrivals walked seven miles through the woods to settle at a place they called German Town.

Today we recognize Germantown as the first permanent Mennonite settlement in America. The families, numbering thirty-three souls, also became the forerunners of more than seven million German immigrants in the years following. So great was their number that Benjamin Franklin feared the American colonies might become a German-speaking nation. Three centuries after Germantown's founding, the 52 million Americans of German descent formed the largest single ethnic group in the United States, followed by 44 million Americans of Irish descent, and 40 million whose ancestors came from Britain.

EARLY LIFE IN GERMANTOWN. From its outset, Germantown was meant to be not an agricultural community but a town. Such was the vision of its founder, Francis Daniel Pastorius, and his compatriots. Millers, weavers, shoemakers, papermakers, cabinetmakers, shopkeepers, and farmers gathered together, forming a brand-new, visionary society—part of an innovative Holy Experiment in which no one religious interpretation was deemed the correct one. The new elements of this urban village—its motifs and character—stand in sharp contrast to the political structures and clime of Europe, from which the village folk had emigrated.

One of the best interpretations of this era is a 1983 tri-centennial tribute, *Germantown and its Founders*, by Margaret B. Tinkcom. What follows has been taken in part from her fine descriptions of early Germantown. These Krefeld émigrés "practiced freedom of religion and self government. They lived in peaceful coexistence with many different types of people and they abhorred the subjugation of human beings because of race. They seized the challenge and opportunity open to them in a new land and they were able to fashion a better way of life than they had known in the Old World to their children and the generations that followed" (Tinkcom, iii).

Pastorius was intent on seeing that the right kinds of persons end up in Germantown. They would need to be flexible as well as able to adapt to an utterly alien environment. The

Company should select from the Germanies families "who were more amiable than some other peoples . . . which in this country is a highly necessary quality." Pastorius even named skills, such as farming, carpentry, and tanning, necessary for the common good. He singled out "a dozen Tyrolese to lay low the mighty oak trees" as helpful. He underscored "a disposition to work" as being paramount, adding to this a warning that "any such as expect to spare their hands remain where they are."

The early Germantown settlers were townsmen, desiring to establish their Old World traditions in the New. Pastorius notes, in this regard, that these townspeople were "not too well skilled in the culture of the ground." They did, however, know enough to plant gardens and orchards, grain, and flax, to establish meadows, and to maintain their wood lots.

Early houses were generally one room, with a loft above, built of rubble stone. One example of these homes still exists, as a detached kitchen of the Rittenhouse Homestead, built around 1690.

The original Germantown immigrants included linen weavers, to whom Pastorius credited the town's "most prominent external prosperity . . . to flax raising, spinning and weaving." Germantown textiles were known far and wide for their superior qualities, not only during the Colonial era, but in the nineteenth century as well.

Papermaking in Colonial America had its beginnings in Germantown. In 1690 William Rittenhouse built a flourishing paper mill along the Wissahickon. Printing and publishing, too, brought Germantown into the center of Colonial intellectual activity. In 1738, Christopher Sauer began what would turn into the largest typographical enterprise in the British colonies.

Religion played a central role in Germantown from the beginning. Lutheran Pietism combined with a Quaker spirit within the souls of the founders. Many who now were Quaker had come from the Mennonite tradition, bringing with them elements of their Mennonite faith and teachings. Lensen remained Mennonite. Abraham Op den Graeff became a Mennonite, probably at the time the Mennonites organized formally as a congregation, around 1698. Mennonites, along with Quakers, had at first come together in homes. Then in 1686 they probably began meeting, together with Quakers, in the new log *Kirchlein* (little church). Soon thereafter the Mennonites also met by themselves, in the house of Isaac van Bebber.

A common thread running through most of the faiths present in Germantown has to do with mutual tolerance. To quote Stephanie Grauman Wolf, "the religious beliefs of most of the early settlers, whether Quaker, Mennonite, or Pietist, put stress on the inner light, on the necessity of individual solutions to religious problems rather than reliance on group experience and ritual" (Wolf, 206-07).

Education was another essential early Germantown element. In 1702, a school opened with Pastorius as teacher. After his death in 1719, Mennonites, Lutherans, and Moravians set up schools. Individual schoolmasters, "advertis[ing] their expertise in the Philadelphia newspapers, offered an even greater

variety, proposing to instruct those interested in practical sub-
jects like surveying and English, as well as in the pleasant arts of
drawing and music" (Tinkcom, 11—but see also ii, 2, 3, 5, 10).

THREE EARLY GERMANTOWNERS DESCRIBE THEIR CULTURE
AND LIFE. Three accounts of life in Germantown during its first
decade of existence are significant enough to be quoted at this
point in our story.

Cornelis Bom's description of the character of early town
life in Germantown expresses well the flavor of a settlement just
three or four years in the making. The Dutchman Bom, by
trade a baker (d. 1689), was the only known Mennonite in
Germantown to have owned a slave:

> I have here a shop of many kinds of goods and edibles.
> Sometimes I ride out with merchandise, and sometimes
> bring something back, mostly from the Indians, and
> deal with them in many things. I have no regular ser-
> vants except one Negro whom I bought. I have no rent,
> no tax, or excise to pay.
>
> I have a cow which gives plenty of milk, a horse to
> ride around, my pigs increase so rapidly so that in the

summer I had seventeen when at first I had only two. I have many chickens and geese, and a garden, and shall next year have an orchard if I am well, so that my wife and I are in good spirits, and are reaching a condition of ease and prosperity in which we have great hopes. But when we first came it was pretty hard in many respects.

Those who come now come in the summer . . . since now everything can be bought with money. The market is supplied with fresh mutton and beef at reasonable price in a way I would not have thought would have occurred in so short a time. Sometimes there is a good supply of partridges for half a stiver [2 ½ cents] a piece, pigeons, ducks, teal, and fish in great quantities in their seasons. There are not many roads to bring to and receive from market, but these things are now beginning to get in order.

In a few years, if it continues in the same way, every thing will be more plentiful than in other lands. The commerce and trade are close to the door to the Barbadoes, Bermudas and other West Indie islands, that will bring this country into good condition. Time will best show this to be the case.

Nevertheless I do not advise anyone to come here. Those who come ought to come after Christian deliberation with pure intentions in the fear of the Lord, so that the Lord may be their support; for before a man here reaches ease he must exercise patience, resignation, and industry, the one as much as the other.

Therefore, whosoever comes here, let him come with the constant mind, having his eyes fixed upon the commands of the God above him. This none can do except those who have the Lord with them in the matter, and are so cleansed from the fleshly and worldly views and they have good counsel in all things" (*Smith*, 91).

The Indians of whom Cornelis Bom speaks intermingled with the newly arrived settlers, as may be seen in an account written around 1693 by Francis Daniel Pastorius:

> [The Indians] are entirely candid, keep to their promises, and deceive and mislead nobody. They are hospitable and are true, and often live together quietly. Their huts are made of bent saplings which they cover with bark. They use neither table nor bench, and have no furniture, except a pot in which they cook their meat. . . . I thought to myself, these wild people have never heard the teachings of Jesus concerning temperance and moderation in their whole lives, and yet observe them much better than Christians. . . .
>
> In our meeting they are very still and attentive, so that I firmly believe at the day of judgment, they will sit above those of Tyre and Sidon and put to shame mere name-and-mouth Christians. . . . They plant about their huts Indian corn and beans, but pay no attention to further cultivation of the ground, and to cattle, and wonder much that the Christians are so much troubled over eating and drinking, clothing and houses, as though they doubted that God would care for them. . . .
>
> They are much better contented with, and more careless about, the future than are we Christians. They circumvent nobody in trade or conduct. They know nothing of the proud manner and modes of dress, to which we adhere. They do not swear and curse. . . . During my ten years here I have never heard of their using force toward anybody, much less committing murder. . . .

Another early town resident, Richard Fraeme, described Germantown in 1692, some nine years after its founding, within the confines of a folksy poem:

> The German-Town of which I spake before,
> Which is at least in length a Mile or more
> Where lives High German People, and Low Dutch
> Where trade in weaving Linnin Cloth is much,
> There grows the Flax, as also you may know,

That from the same they do divide the Tow.
Their Trade fits well within this Habitation,
We find convenience for their Occupation,
One Trade brings in imployement for another,
So that we may suppose each Trade a Brother;
From Linnin Rags good Paper doth derive,
The first Trade keeps the second Trade alive;
Without the first the second cannot be,
Therefore since these two can so well agree,
Convenience doth approve to place them nigh,
One in the Germantown, together hard by.
A Paper Mill near German-Town doth stand,
So that Flax, which first springs from the Land,
First Flax, then Yarn, then they must begin,
To weave the same, which they took pains to spin.
Also when on our backs it is well worn,
Some of the same remains Ragged and Torn;
Then of the Rags our Paper it is made,
Which in process of time doth waste and fade;
So what comes from the Earth, appeareth plain,
The same in Time returns to Earth again. (*Smith*, 92)

After 1700, the influx of urban Dutch and Low Country
German immigrants declined, replaced largely with rural Swiss
immigrants, who settled on farms upcountry in what is today
the Franconia Mennonite area. Here lies one reason why, after
the Mennonites organized as a congregation in 1698, they
never exceeded fifteen percent of the total Germantown population at any time in its history, even though many of the original families that came to Germantown were Mennonite in
origin. A few years later, other rural Swiss Mennonite and
Amish immigrants took up stakes in what is today the Lancaster area.

Some of the qualities that made Germantown non-rural in
nature—and in this sense proto-urban and then urban in the
fullest sense of the term—become visible in the following pré-
cis of Tinkcom and Wolf's observations (as quoted above): di-

versity, flexibility, the importance of education, commercial development, freedom of religion, living in peaceful coexistence with many different types of people, abhorring the subjugation of human beings because of race, "neighbors, also offer[ing] each other a kind and helping hand," the respect for the Almighty. Germantowners were "highly mobile and heterogeneous." Their education included "the pleasant arts of drawing and music." They emphasized the individual inner light in contending with questions of faith, rather than relying too heavily on congregational dynamics and ecclesiastical ritual, as carried by the established churches of Europe.

However, as a social totality, those who comprised the village of Germantown worked in harmony in areas of the common good, no matter their religious persuasion. They took the initiative in promoting and living out the way of peace and good will, and in protesting against injustice. One such protest against injustice came in the year 1688, and merits its own subsection, leading to a deeper understanding of how some Germantowners measured human worth.

THE ANTI-SLAVERY PETITION OF 1688. The first-known slavery protest in British Colonial America goes back to Germantown in the year 1688. (As eaerlier noted, Mennonite opposition to slavery in the 1663 Dutch Plockhoy community, in what is today the state of Delaware, was a quarter-century prior.) This significant slavery protest was composed by four men, a Lutheran pietist and three Quaker-Mennonites, who joined hands to protest the "traffik of men-body," then a widespread reality in many North American colonies. In the name of the Ten Commandments (on adultery, and on stealing), in the name of the Golden Rule of Jesus (Matt. 7:12), and in the very name of Christianity itself, the protesters built their case.

Although three of the four who signed this protest were Quakers at the time—there would not be an organized Mennonite congregation in Germantown until 1698—three of the signers had been Mennonite. One signer, Abraham Op den Graeff, became Mennonite formally, once the congregation organized. Yet again we see at the heart of this petition an urban phenomenon: a certain concern for justice—something that Low Country Mennonites were equal to, but something the later, rural Swiss who moved up-country were less inclined to be involved in, at least in responding to injustices through this manner of protest. Here are a few excerpts from the 1688 protest statement:

> . . . Now, though they are black, we cannot conceive there is more liberty to have them slaves, as it is to have other white ones.
>
> There is a saying that we shall do to all men like as we will be done ourselves—making no difference of what generation, descent or color they are. And those who steal or rob men, and those who buy or purchase them, are they not alike? Here [in this land] is liberty of conscience which is right and reasonable; here ought to be likewise liberty of the body, except of evil-doers, which is another case. But to bring men hither, or to rob and sell them against their will, we stand against. In Europe, there are many oppressed for conscience sake; and here there are those oppressed, who are of a black color.
>
> And we who know that men must not commit adultery—some do commit adultery in others, separating wives from their husbands and giving them to others; and some sell the children of these poor creatures to other men. Ah! Do consider well this thing, you who do it, if you would be done at this manner? And if it is done according to Christianity? . . .
>
> And we who profess that it is not lawful to steal, must, likewise, avoid to purchase such things as are stolen, but rather help to stop this robbing and stealing if possible. And such men ought to be delivered out of the hands of the robbers, and set free as well as in Europe. . . .

If once these slaves (which they say are so wicked and stubborn men) should point themselves—fight for their freedom—and handle their masters and mistresses as they did handle them before; will these masters and mistresses take the sword at hand and war against these poor slaves, like, we are able to believe, some will not refuse to do; or have these Negroes not as much right to fight for their freedom, as you have to keep them slaves?

Now consider well this thing, if it is good or bad? And in case you find it to be good to handle these blacks at that manner, we desire and require you hereby lovingly that you may inform us herein, which at this time never was done, namely, that Christians have such a liberty to do so. . . .

This is from our meeting at Germantown [Pennsylvania], held the eighteenth of the second month, 1688, to be delivered to the Monthly Meeting at Richard Worrell's. [Signed,] Gerrit Hendricks, Derick op den Graff, Francis Daniel Pastorius and Abraham op den Graff. [The "second" month on the Quaker calendar is actually April.]

THE BATTLE OF GERMANTOWN. The Colonial Era came to an end in the 1770s, when a rise in the desire for independence from British rule precipitated the Revolutionary War. At one point in the war, Germantown found itself in the very heat of battle.

During the night of Friday, October 3, 1777, George Washington ordered his army of underfed, ill-clothed, and mostly barefoot soldiers to break camp in the Skippack and Perkiomen valleys—where they had been engaged in two weeks of senseless destruction—to march on the British at Germantown. The Americans were instructed to reach Germantown from four different directions by 5:00 a.m., just before sunrise.

Three of the groups arrived on time; one, led by General Smallwood, got lost along the way. Precisely at 5:00 the Americans rushed down the main street of Germantown. For two and a half hours that Saturday morning Germantown resounded with the roar of cannons and guns, shouts of command, and the screams of the dying, as every house, hedge, and garden was bitterly contested. Just beyond the new Mennonite meeting-house, built in 1770, stood the home of Jakob Keyser, who with his son John went out to care for the wounded from both armies.

In one instance, the Americans mistakenly fired on each other, adding to the confusion. The British general Agnew was toppled from his horse by a shot fired from the Mennonite cemetery. Elizabeth Engel watched from her doorway as several men carried the mortally wounded general past her house. Finally the Americans retreated, leaving behind 152 dead, 521 wounded, and more than 400 captives. The British admitted to losing half that many.

The Mennonites, Quakers, and Brethren tried to remain neutral in the conflict. They were therefore regarded with mistrust by both sides. "If one objects with a mere word, one is told: You are a Tory," wrote Henry Mühlenberg in his diary: "Those on the other side say: You are rebels." Washington, now encamped near Pennypacker's Mill, and mindful of the approaching winter, ordered the "collection" of blankets, stockings and clothing from the civilians, adding that "It is especially *recommended* to get these things from the Quakers and other dissatisfied inhabitants . . . the point is, by all means, to get *them*." No wonder that some Mennonites in eastern Pennsylvania would soon set their sights on a new beginning in Upper Canada (now Ontario).

The Battle of Germantown was a far cry from the spirit and substance of William Penn's Holy Experiment. Whatever happened to this idea, largely realized, of a peaceable kingdom here and now? The Holy Experiment had worked—that is, for about three generations, at which point the Quakers were slowly but surely eased out of their central role in Colonial

Pennsylvania policy making; in their stead appeared "realists," who threatened retaliation through the force of gunfire, if need be—contrary to the Quaker, Brethren, and Mennonite way. This new breed of political leadership increased in power until it ultimately gained upper hand.

DID THE HOLY EXPERIMENT ULTIMATELY FAIL? The answer is both yes and no. The joining of hands—of the peace churches and of the state—was attempted, and *this* form of the Holy Experiment came to an end.

Yet the basic idea of the Holy Experiment itself lives to this day in the communal lives of the followers of the Historic Peace Churches. The Church of the Brethren, the Quakers and the Mennonites continue to affirm with conviction their heritage of peace and the quest for social justice. To be sure, many others from, a number of other religious traditions as well, have rested their faith and actions on this foundation of Christ's gospel of peace.

GERMANTOWN AFTER THE COLONIAL ERA. After the Revolutionary War, which brought the Colonial Era to an end, Germantown continued to grow and broaden culturally. We close this section with a quote from Margaret Tinkcom, who takes our story succinctly through the next century:

> By 1800, the community could be called an "urban village." . . . This diversity only accelerated during the nineteenth century when trains and streetcars connected the . . . town with center city Philadelphia, and new factories spewed smoke over former farmlands. Commercial development and the construction of large apartment houses during the twentieth century have made Germantown what it is today: a fully urbanized section of the City of Philadelphia. (Tinkcom, iii)

II

The Colonial
𝕲𝖊𝖗𝖒𝖆𝖓𝖙𝖔𝖜𝖓
Mennonites, Pictorially

The Indians and William Penn. It has been said that Penn enjoyed trusting and friendly relations with the Native Americans.

The Concord. In 1983 the U.S. post office and the German postal services jointly issued an identical stamp commemorating the three-hundredth anniversary of the voyage of the Concord.

Francis Daniel Pastorius. Pastorius, himself a Lutheran, played a significant role in bringing the Mennonites to Germantown.

The "Weberdenkmal." The Weaver Monument in Krefeld (Lower Rhine), Germany, commemorates the departure of the Mennonite weavers to America.

The William Rittenhouse Homestead. The Rittenhouse Homestead is located along the Wissahickon Drive through Fairmont Park, Philadelphia.

Rittenhouse Oath of Citizenship. This document, dated 1679, establishes Rittenhouse as a citizen of Amsterdam, Holland.

The Fireplace. This clearly illustrates the generous size of the hearth in the oldest building on the Rittenhouse property, built around 1690.

The Stairway. This divided stairway is a unique feature of the Rittenhouse Homestead.

The Rittenhouse Plaque. This plaque, located slightly upstream from the home-stead, marks the site of the first paper mill in Colonial America.

The Johnson House, on the corner of Washington Lane and Germantown Avenue, stands virtually unchanged since the days of its construction by Jakob Knorr in the 1760s.

The Wyck House is the oldest house on Germantown Avenue, the original section built by Hans Milan around 1690.

The Wyck House, the pump outside.

The Wyck House, interior.

*The Concord School was completed by Jakob
Knorr in 1775. The second story was added in
1818.*

The Concord School. Two views of its interior.

The Upper (Axe's) Burial Ground. This burial site is located next to the Concord School. The oldest known stone dates back to 1716; the last interment took place in 1907.

Father (Johannes) Kelpius' Cave. The cave where the mystic Johannes Kelpius came to meditate is located in Hermit's Glen, at the north end of Fairmont Park.

The Germantown Mennonite Meetinghouse, built in 1770.

Slavery Protest Table. Oral tradition has it that the Slavery Petition of 1688 was signed on this table, in the home of Quaker-Mennonite Thones Kunders.

Cut Nails. These original nails were removed from the Meetinghouse at the time of a recent re-roofing

Germantown Mennonite Meetinghouse, interior, c. 1975.

Bench from pre-1770 Meetinghouse, still in use today.

The peace in Germantown was shattered early on October 4, 1777, when George Washington and his army engaged the British in hours-long battle. Because Mennonites, Quakers, and Brethren tried to remain neutral in the conflict, they were mistrusted by both parties.

The 1857 Mennonite Meetinghouse fence along Germantown Avenue.

*Church of the Brethren Meetinghouse. The Brethren Meetinghouse
was also built in 1770, with later additions in 1896 and 1915.*

*Site of First Brethren Baptism in North America. Located along the
Wissahickon Creek, this marks the spot where the first Brethren bap-
tisms took place on Christmas day, 1723.*

Above: *The Christopher Sauer Home. The Sauer Press, on the corner of Germantown Avenue and Bowman's Lane (today, Queen Lane), printed and published the first European language Bibles in the New World.* ***Below:*** *Christopher Sauer and Alexander Mack Signatures. The Sauer and Mack families were significant leaders in the Germantown community.*

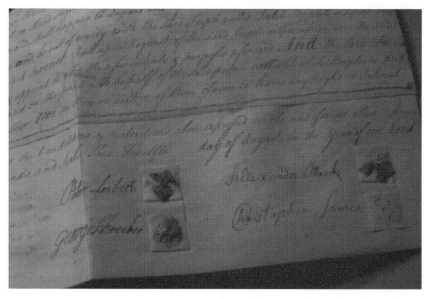

Germantown stoops. Much of historical Germantown remains to this day.

Germantown Avenue, 1985, when the trolleys were still running. Germantown Avenue (the whole of the Colonial Germantown Historic District, including the Mennonite Meetinghouse, Wyck House, the Johnson House, and Concord School) is the only historic street in America recognized and so listed on the National Register of Historic Places. Furthermore, it is one of only 152 sites in all of Pennsylvania to be granted the coveted designation of "National Historic Landmark."

III

Tour Guide

This section details historic Germantown sites still in existence that held significance for Mennonites and Brethren. These short descriptions all relate in some fashion to Mennonite and Brethren beginnings in the New World, within the context of the larger Colonial Quaker story. A detailed map of the Germantown area including Fairmount Park, useful for a walking and/or driving tour, completes the section.

THE RITTENHOUSE HOMESTEAD. The Rittenhouse Homestead, one of the oldest remaining edifices in Germantown, symbolizes the life and faith of the first generation of Germantown Mennonite settlers. Nestled in a valley among the trees of Fairmont Park, this is the home of William Rittenhouse (Willem Rittinghuysen). Born in Germany but a naturalized citizen of Amsterdam (The Netherlands), Rittenhouse and his family arrived in Germantown in 1688. With his son Nikolaas and three other partners, William built a paper mill on a tributary of the Wissahickon. This mill produced the first paper made in the American colonies. Rittenhouse was elected to be the first minister of the Germantown congregation and continued to serve in this position till his death in 1708.

Floods washed out the mill on two occasions; the second time it was not rebuilt. Still standing are the original home and outbuildings, built in typical Palatine German style with steep roofs, narrow casement windows, and Dutch doors. The original home, later used as a detached kitchen, may have been built as early as 1690, and a new home in 1707, with an addition in 1713. One can well imagine lively Mennonite *Versammlungen* (meetings) being held in these quarters in these early years.

As already noted in the historical section, research suggests that "the first houses were small, most probably no more than one room with a loft above, rather like the detached kitchen of the Rittenhouse house, the best existing example of this early plan. Like it, they were often built of rubble stone," more than likely taken from the bed of the Wissahickon.

Home, vocation and faith—and the expressions thereof from the vantage point of the Mennonites—can find fulfillment only when correlated with each other, and with all other spheres that entail life. It is here that the Rittenhouse Homestead takes on its deepest significance, where these spheres found their true interaction in a homestead, where enterprise was exercised, and where Mennonite worship took place.

THE GERMANTOWN MENNONITE MEETINGHOUSE.[1] Evidence points quite clearly to the hillside which ran back from the lot now occupied by the church and cemetery as the place where the first Mennonite settlers built their temporary shelters for the oncoming winter. There was a fine running spring at the foot of this hill, a delightful landmark still in the memory of people living at the beginning of the twentieth century—but since disposed of through drains underneath the houses and streets, on the north side of East Herman Street.

Here in these temporary houses, the pioneers began holding meetings in united worship, though they had as yet no ordained minister among them. The house occupied by Quaker-Mennonite Thones Kunders, one of the leaders of the new community, is generally spoken of as the place where these meetings were held. It must have been here in his first house, not in his later-built stone house fully a mile further down the road, that these worship services were held.

A little over a month after their arrival, sorrow came to their little community. Herman op den Graeff wrote in a letter to his friends back in Krefeld, "My mother died on November nineteenth and was buried in this very place." Thus begins the history of this spot as a burying ground.

Being thus consecrated, this lot became the obvious place for the first meetinghouse in Germantown. Francis Daniel Pastorius, the most prominent Germantown leader, writes in a report, "We have here in Germantown, in the year 1686, built a little meetinghouse for the *Gemeinde* (community), not with a view to an outwardly large stone structure, but that the temple of God (which we believers ourselves are) may be built up and all of us be nurtured in holiness and a godly life." This statement suggests that the meetinghouse, constructed on lot Nr. 4, was built for the common use of Mennonites and others.

The congregation, although active, still was without a minister. A year later, William Rittenhouse arrived in Germantown from Amsterdam, Holland. He bought fifty acres of land from Peter Keurlis on September 6, 1687, recorded as Lot No. 19. In 1698 the congregation organized, electing him as the lead minister, with Jan Nyce (Neuss) as Deacon. Dirk Keyser, who came the same year as Rittenhouse, was also recognized as a minister in the congregation. In 1702 two more ministers were chosen, Jacob Gottschalk (Gaetschalck) and Hans Nyce (Neuss). Moves were made to have Rittenhouse ordained as *Ältester* (lead minister). However, he died before the ordination was to take place. Here, then, we see the formal beginning of the Mennonite church in North America.

In 1701, William Rittenhouse conveyed part of lot No.19, fronting on Main Street, to Arnold van Fossen. He in turn, on February 16, 1702, conveyed that parcel to Jan Nyce (Neuss) as trustee, on behalf of the Mennonites. Their intent was to establish a cemetery, school and meetinghouse. In this manner the site came into the legal possession of the Germantown Mennonite congregation. In 1714, a further part of this lot, containing 35 square perches (about 10,000 square feet), was conveyed to Henry Sellen and Jan Nyce as trustees for the Mennonites. These two land acquisitions were to provide "for a place to erect a meeting house for the use and service of the sd Mennonists (: alias Menisten :) and for a place to bury their dead," with the deed distinctly restricting its use for the Mennonite church and cemetery forever.

Although the exact dates are not clear, around this time, the growing congregation acted on these transfers of lands by constructing a meetinghouse for its own use. It served both for church and school purposes. It was in this building that Christopher Dock, "the pious schoolmaster of the Skippack," taught school during the 1730s. According to oral tradition, two pieces of furniture used in his school, the teacher's table and one of the long benches, are preserved and still in use in the church. The table has the further distinction that, according to oral tradition, on it was signed the first formal protest against slavery in North America, in 1688.

The log meetinghouse served the congregation well for over half a century, until in 1770 it gave way to the more durable stone building which stands on the same grounds and is still in a good state of preservation. In 1908 an annex in matching style and material was added, during the pastorate of J. W. Bayley.

A record of the cost of the 1770 building was made by the Mennonite builder Jacob Knorr, whose personal bill for the carpenter work was £39 s12, of which he personally deducted the sum of £9 s10. The entire cost of the building came to £202 s5, which in the 1920s was calculated to be about $1,000. The same records show that some materials from the old building were used.

By 1712, the congregation had grown, numbering 99 members, and extended all the way to Skippack. But it was not long till the Franconia Mennonite country settlements organized churches for themselves, and Germantown became the lesser among a growing number of congregations. There came a time when there was no minister left in Germantown, and the services were supplied by ministers from the country congregations.

The Germantown congregation experienced many ups and downs, ranging in membership from almost a hundred to no more than ten, most of whom no longer actually lived in Germantown.

In the early 1970s there was a turnaround, eventuating in a rapidly growing congregation numbering over a hundred. This ultimately necessitated the search for larger and more flexible facilities. By 1986 the congregation had outgrown the Meetinghouse and moved to rented facilities for eight years. In 1994 they moved to their present facilities on nearby Washington Lane.

The 1770 Meetinghouse still stands as a memento and symbol of the presence of the oldest ongoing Mennonite congregation in North America. The first Mennonite funerals; wedding, baptismal, and communion services; and the first expressions of concern for peace and social justice occurred at this historic Germantown location. In 1725 the first Mennonite conference in America was held, possibly here in the previous meetinghouse, at which time the Dordrecht Confession of Faith was adopted. The title page of this first English-language edition shows it was published in Germantown.

The stone Meetinghouse of 1770, in addition to its rich historical interest, holds high architectural interest as a prime example of Mennonite religious architecture. In line with Mennonite belief, "church" is the people of the congregation rather than the house where they meet.

Consequently, Mennonites historically chose a simple, unadorned structure with little exterior ornamentation, without steeple, bells, crosses, or stained glass windows. The eighteenth-century exterior reflects this ideal with its simple symmetrical style and the use of unpretentious local stone, a style often called Germantown Georgian. The austere interior with simple pulpit, table, and benches served a people gathered for non-liturgical worship, preaching, prayer, song. This style would be repeated in many Mennonite congregations scattered throughout Pennsylvania and across the expanding frontiers. As a part of the Germantown Avenue historic district, the Meetinghouse stands on the National Register of Historic Places. The Meetinghouse and area are also designated as a National Historic Landmark by the National Park Service.

THE WYCK HOUSE. The oldest house on Germantown Avenue is the Wyck House. The original part was built by Hans Milan, around 1690. Little is known about Milan, whose surname later appears among Mennonites further west. Soon thereafter, a separate house was built directly east of the Milan house for Milan's daughter and her new husband, Dirck Jansen. Later, the two homes were joined together, creating the large Wyck House as it appears today. Jansen's daughter Catherine married Casper Wister, whose daughter married Reuben Haines. For six generations, the home was in the hands of this family of Quakers, the Haines, till 1973, when Mrs. Robert Haines III, last family owner of Wyck, turned over the Wyck property deed to the Wyck Charitable Trust. The Wyck Committee has oversight over the house. Six generations of the same Quaker family is a record with few parallels in the history of Great American Homes.

Wyck has thus over the centuries continually exemplified first Mennonite and then Quaker standards and values. Both the great and the humble have experienced friendship and hospitality at Wyck. Tradition has it that Indians knew they were welcome in the Wyck House in the heart of winter, entering the kitchen unannounced, to be given food and a warm drink, with shared greetings around a cozy fireplace. Wyck's spacious lawns and its attractive garden have won acclaim for generations. And over the decades there have been ties of friendship between the Quaker residents of Wyck and their neighbors at the Germantown Mennonite Meetinghouse.

Wyck House is located one block south of the Mennonite Meetinghouse on two-and-a-half acres of land, on the corner of Germantown Avenue and Walnut Lane, a remnant of the original twenty acres of wooded property. Also on the premises are a smokehouse, a carriage house, and an icehouse. The barn, built in 1796 and still standing, is no longer part of the Wyck property. The garden is important because of its old-fashioned roses, rare shrubs, fruit trees, and herbs, placed according to plans sketched out in old family papers. On the National Register of Historic Places—as are a number of other historic homes on the avenue—a visit to Wyck is well worth one's time. The whole spectrum of Quaker cultural history comes alive before one's eyes.

THE JOHNSON HOUSE. Located along Germantown Avenue, on the corner of the old Abingdon Road, stands the Johnson House, a striking example of Colonial Germantown architecture. The house was built by the Mennonite builder Jakob Knorr between 1765 and 1768 for a Quaker, John Johnson (Jan Jansen), who presented the home as a wedding present to his son.

John Johnson Jr., a tanner by trade, was a direct descendant of the pioneer settler Dirck Jansen, possibly of Quaker-Mennonite origins. John Junior and his family lived here, enjoying the peacefulness of Germantown and living in peace with their Quaker/Mennonite/Brethren neighbors.

In the early morning of October 4, 1777, that peace was rudely disturbed when George Washington's rag-tag army of patriots marched through town to attack the British in Philadelphia. Concentrated fighting broke out and quickly engulfed the new stone meetinghouse of the Mennonites, the Johnson house, and the other homes along Germantown Avenue. The patriots commandeered most of the Johnson family's food supplies, but the family offered no resistance, remembering that Christ's teaching did not allow them to fight for one's property. The scars of the Battle of Germantown are still visible on the building.

Perhaps of greater significance, at least for American social history in general, and Quaker and Mennonite history in particular, is the significance of the Johnson House as an Underground Railroad stop during the pre-Civil War era. Germantown was a prominent site on the Underground Railroad, and black people fleeing from bondage would cross the Schuylkill River at Flat Rock Dam, come along the Wissahickon, and lodge in Germantown before proceeding further to Dreshertown. The Quakers and Mennonites of Germantown, knowing slavery to be a sin against God, assisted the black community in sheltering these fugitives. This particular corner in Germantown was well used, as the Johnsons, the Nyces, and the Knorrs all took a hand in the work. Usually it was a Johnson who drove the fugitives to their next destination.

The Johnson House is the only building in Philadelphia that was part of the Underground Railroad, still in its original state. Other such sites exist in Philadelphia, but their specific role in the Underground Railroad drama cannot be as accurately identified as the Johnson House.

For two-thirds of a century the Johnson House was owned and managed by the Women's Club of Germantown, an organization 600 strong, to create a force for the good in the social, civic, educational and philanthropic life of Germantown. For their regular meetings and other functions, the Women's Club of Germantown erected in 1922, at the far end of the Johnson House garden, a large modern assembly building in matching style, suitable for stage plays, banquets and meetings. In 1992 this building was acquired by the Germantown Mennonite Church to be their new center of worship and activities, and after two years of renovation they moved in.

In 1980 the Women's Club donated the well-preserved Johnson House to the Germantown Mennonite Church Corporation (today, the Germantown Mennonite Historic Trust).

The Mennonites in turn deeded it in 2003 to an African-American organization, the Johnson House Historic Site Board, as a museum of black history.

THE CONCORD SCHOOLHOUSE. Education was always an important part in the life of the Quakers, Mennonites, and Brethren in Germantown. A school for the Dutch-German immigrants was begun less than a decade after their arrival, in 1702, by Francis Daniel Pastorius. In later years, Christopher Dock, the Mennonite schoolmaster from Skippack, spent four summers in Germantown, presumably teaching in the wood-framed meetinghouse. Twenty years after his death, his book on education, *Schul-Ordnung* (School Management), was published by Christopher Saur II, whose age would suggest he may well have been one of Dock's Germantown students.

Steps toward establishing a new school, to be named Concord, began in March 1775, when residents of Upper Germantown met to discuss the need for a school closer to their homes. The Union School in Lower Germantown had begun classes in 1759, providing an English education for the Germantown students. However, "taking into consideration the distance and particular inconvenience through the winter season of sending their children to the Lower School," the residents of Upper Germantown decided to operate their own school. (The Union School—at what is today 110 West School House Lane, just off Germantown Avenue—was about one mile distant.)

By autumn 1775 the building, constructed by the Mennonite architect-builder Jakob Knorr, was completed. The new structure filled with sounds of anticipation, as students eager to learn met with their new schoolmaster, John Grimes. Located on a corner of the Upper Burial Ground, across the street from the Johnson House, and two blocks north of the Mennonite Meetinghouse, the school was ideally located for the Mennonite families of Germantown, many of whom played an active role in this subscription school.

The original school building was one-and-a-half stories high. Around 1818 the trustees decided to "raise the roof" of the Concord School, making it two-and-a-half stories high, to provide meeting space for local organizations such as literary societies and singing schools. In 1855 the Charter Oak Library and Literary Association installed their library on the second floor, taking an active role in the social and intellectual life of the community for well over half a century.

From its slight elevation overlooking Germantown Avenue, Concord School continued in the tradition of providing a good education for the children of Germantown. The School still stands in its pristine state, exuding the flavor of a bygone era of education—ink wells, benches, the original schoolmaster's desk, the old water pump. One can almost hear the sounds of yesteryear reverberating from the walls.

Legend has it that the heavy center beam supporting the main floor formerly served as a mast of the ship, *Concord*, which brought the first settlers here in 1683. The Concord school bell was brought to Philadelphia on the British tea ship *Polly*, which was not permitted to land and to unload. The ship went back to Great Britain, then returned to Philadelphia after the war, at which time the bell was finally unloaded, delivered, and installed.

The Concord Schoolhouse is one of the few remaining Colonial one-room schoolhouses, with no running water (only the old-fashioned pump outside), no indoor bathroom (only an outhouse in the back yard), no electricity (natural lighting by day, candle-power by night—with each person bringing his or her own candle), and only a fireplace (plus later a potbelly stove) as the source of heat in winter.

THE UPPER BURIAL GROUND. Just north of and adjacent to the Concord School is the Upper Burial Ground, also known as the Axe's Burial Ground. In 1692, nine years after the founding of Germantown, both the Upper and the Lower Burial Grounds were created by a deed from Paul Wulff. Each cemetery had its own board of trustees who kept separate records.

Among the Upper Burial Ground's records, we find a list of the contributors to the expense of constructing a stone wall along Germantown Avenue that was completed in spring 1724. The three remaining sides of the grounds were walled in, in matching style, in 1760.

The oldest known stone is the one of the Mennonite settler Cornelius Tyson, who arrived in 1683 and died in 1716 at the age of sixty-three. Other stones mark the graves of the Knorrs and other pioneer families as well as the graves of Indians who died while encamped in and around Germantown.

Three officers and five soldiers of George Washington's army also lie buried there. Also there is Germantown's own Methuselah, Adam Shisler, who died in 1777 at the age of 969—a stonecutter's mistake!

Altogether there have been around 1300 burials on the grounds, with the last interment taking place in 1907. The last surviving trustee of the Upper Burial Ground died in 1943. Two years later the Courts of Philadelphia placed the two historic properties, the Concord School (built 1775) and the Upper Burial Ground (established 1692) under the jurisdiction of a single board of trustees.

FATHER KELPIUS' CAVE. In 1694 Johannes Kelpius, son of a Lutheran pastor, led a group of about forty German religious enthusiasts from Germany to America to settle at Germantown, a place he believed to be a spiritual paradise in an unspoiled wilderness. Kelpius spent many hours meditating in caves along the rugged, densely wooded banks overlooking the Wissahickon. His special cave is located in Hermit's Glen at the north end of Fairmount Park. Today Kelpius' cave is listed as one of Philadelphia's historic landmarks.

Although he was somewhat of a recluse, Kelpius sought to appropriate the best elements of each of the religious groups, including the Mennonites, with whom he was familiar. He tried to unite these virtues into one harmonious, universal Christian religion. He was troubled by the hypocrisy and strife among Christians in particular and by the godlessness of society in general. In his writings Kelpius often decried the low state to which Christianity had fallen.

Kelpius was by nature a mystic, and there is evidence that he spent increasing amounts of time in caves, contemplating the return of Christ. His apocalyptic and ascetic inclinations seem to have deepened steadily from about 1700 until his death in 1708 at age thirty-five.

Shortly after his death, Kelpius' band of followers disintegrated. A portrait of Kelpius, painted by Christopher Witt, is said to be the oldest surviving American oil painting.

THE BRETHREN MEETINGHOUSE. In 1719 a large number of Brethren refugees from the town of Schwarzenau and environs, in the Sauerland of Germany, departed from Hellevoetsluis, Holland, destined for Germantown. In 1729 a second group left Surhuisterveen, Friesland (The Netherlands), under the leadership of Alexander Mack. A few other migrations in 1730 completed the exodus from Europe, so that the whole Brethren movement from this time on was North American.

The Brethren, close spiritual cousins to the Mennonites and Quakers, are the third branch of the Historic Peace Churches. In Europe, the Brethren often had settled next door to the Mennonites, and in many instances, found support and refuge among them. In fact a number of the Brethren had Anabaptist roots, although they, with others out of the Protestant tradition, found spiritual renewal and kinship within the Pietism that was in the air throughout much of central Europe at the time.

The first group of immigrants (1719) carried with them the seeds of differences that had surfaced during their years in the Lower Rhineland. These had to do with church governance and with marriage. The difficulties of getting established in a new and unsettled land contributed to this disunity, which surfaced in crisis proportions in the New World. By 1722 Peter Becker and other brethren made a valiant effort to bring the Brethren into closer fellowship.

Meetings were begun that winter, alternating between the homes of Becker and Hans Gumre (John Gomorry). In 1723, on Christmas Day, a special event took place: the baptism of six individuals in the Wissahickon (near Kitchen's Lane in Fairmount Park), followed by a love feast in the home of John Gomorry for the twenty-three members present. This event is generally seen as a new beginning for the Church of the Brethren. Today a bronze plaque, marking the site of the first baptism, draws many visitors.

After the 1730s, the Brethren in Germantown also experienced a decrease in membership, when many left for the more rural areas up-country. Also, the clarion call to Christian perfection led a number of Brethren to what became the Ephrata Cloister, at Ephrata, Pennsylvania. This separate Brethren movement, founded in 1732 by Conrad Beissel, embraced Sabbatarianism (Saturday as the Sabbath) and celibacy, although the group also included married householders. By 1750, the Cloister's population was around 300. After 1770 the community declined until 1814, when the Pennsylvania General Assembly incorporated the "Society of Seventh-Day Baptists of Ephrata," and a board of lay trustees was chosen to administer the community property. In 1934 the state revoked the congregation's charter, and in 1941 it bought the remaining cloister property. Following restoration, Ephrata became a much-visited heritage site. In 1968 it was officially recognized as a National Historic Landmark.

Among the Brethren in Germantown, two men bearing the names of their well-known fathers, Alexander Mack Jr. and Christopher Sauer II, rose to prominence, granting effective leadership for the Brethren congregation. From 1723 to 1760 the group met in homes, then for the next ten years in one room of the Pettikoffer house. Finally, in 1770, the same year the Mennonite Meetinghouse was built, the Brethren too built their Meetinghouse, with later additions in 1896 and 1915.

Membership in the Germantown Brethren Church continued to decline over the decades, and worship services ultimately came to an end. In 1965, the Brethren began a ministry among the African-Americans living in the area. In 1980 church services in the old Meetinghouse were reintroduced.

Many Brethren come to visit their meetinghouse in Germantown, which they recognize as the mother church of the denomination in North America.

CHRISTOPHER SAUER'S PRINT SHOP. Living among the Mennonites and Quakers of Colonial Germantown was the noted printer and publisher Christopher Sauer. In 1738, after some years of pioneering and small-scale farming in the Lancaster area, Sauer began his notable career as the first German language printer and publisher in America. In his weekly newspaper, widely circulated among the Pennsylvania Germans, Christopher spoke out boldly against war, violence, and slavery, as well as for friendly relations with the Indians.

The Sauer Press, located on the corner of Germantown Avenue and Bowman's Lane (today Queen Lane), printed and published the first Bible in the New World in a European language. The same press, later managed by son Christopher Sauer II (a Brethren minister), produced three editions of the Ausbund, two other Mennonite classics, and the writings of the good schoolmaster on the Skippack, Christopher Dock. The elder Sauer and Dock both came to Germantown from Germany and were similar in age. Sauer came from near Laasphe in the Sauerland, not far from where Alexander Mack founded the Church of the Brethren.

The peace-loving Sauers and their press fared badly at the hands of George Washington and his patriots, who had no patience with "stubborn Germans" who refused to fight or to contribute willingly to the war effort. The Sauer house was emptied to the bare walls, then confiscated. Sauer (Christopher II) was only allowed the clothes on his back and—after some pleading—his spectacles. But even cruel treatment and losing everything they had lived and worked for failed to turn the Sauers away from a firm belief in Christ-like nonresistance.

Christopher Sauer I died in 1758, thirty-four years after his arrival in Penn's Woods. His son, Christopher II, took over his father's printing establishment and consciously continued under his father's motto: "For the glory of God and my neighbor's good." Indeed, this has become an informal statement of faith for some Church of the Brethren congregations.

Epilogue

The Mennonites have the honor of being [amongst] the original set-tlers in Germantown. That claim unquestionably belongs to them, for they are given that distinction in every history that details the events pertaining to the early settlement of Germantown. They be-lieve in the doctrine of faith, that it is wrong to take up the sword against [fellow humans]; such a belief was first expressed [during the sixteenth century Reformation] by the Mennonites; and the Quakers followed in their wake. Certain it is that the Mennonites were the first [Reformation group] to champion the cause which had its origin in their conscience, and it was solely through their ef-forts and some [from the Church of the Brethren] (Dunkards) that the Legislature of Pennsylvania intervened and enacted that they and the Quakers should be exempt from military service (Constitu-tion of Pennsylvania, Article I, Declaration of Rights, Section 3).
—Daniel K. Cassel, 1888 (*History of the Mennonites*, 100-101)

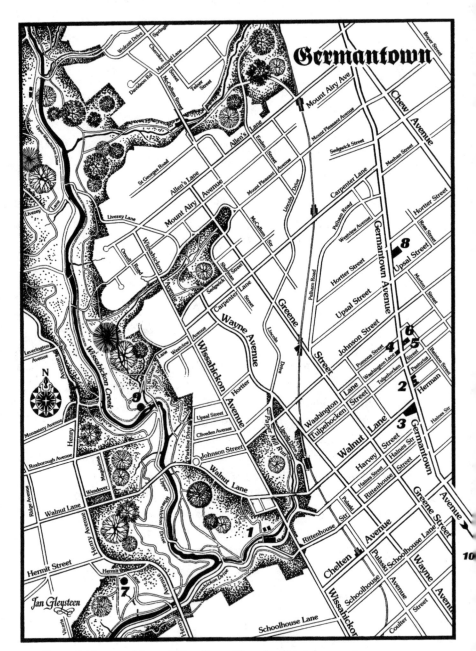

Colonial Mennonite and Brethren Sites in Germantown
1. Rittenhouse Homestead and Rittenhouse Village. 2. Mennonite Meetinghouse, built in 1770. 3. Wyck House. 4. Johnson House. 5. Concord School. 6. Upper Burial Ground. 7. Father Kelpius' Cave. 8. Brethren Meetinghouse, built in 1770. 9. Site of first Brethren baptism in North America. 10. Site of Christopher Sauer's Print Shop

Appendix

An important interpretation of Germantown Mennonite history—which has been a valuable resource in the preparation of this book—was published in 1923, as part of a public invitation to attend special 240th-anniversary weeklong meetings at Germantown. This short history was carefully researched on the basis of original deeds and other rare documentation, and includes details not otherwise readily available. Consequently, much of the booklet is reproduced below as an appendix. (Later research, however, suggests that the minister, William Rittenhouse, although called to be Ältester, died just after receiving from Amsterdam confirmation of his new status, but before he was able to begin carrying out his new duties. Other needed corrections may be found in the text above, which was taken, in part, from this booklet.)

**The 240th Anniversary
of the Coming of the
First Mennonite Pilgrims
and the Founding of Germantown.
A week's program in the
Germantown Mennonite Church
Germantown Avenue above Herman Street
October sixth to thirteenth, 1923**

HISTORIC SKETCH,1683–1923

The history of this place dates back to the year 1683, when the first company of Mennonite pilgrims, who following the invitation of William Penn, landed at Philadelphia. They had secured passage on a vessel named Concord, and sailed from London on July 24th. They arrived at Philadelphia on October 6, 1683.

Here they were received and taken care of by Francis Daniel Pastorius, who, like Penn, had visited them in their home in Crefeld, Germany, and had come over several months ahead of them, having arrived at Philadelphia on August twelfth. He says he cared for twenty women and children in his own dugout at Front and Pine Streets. The men he took out to a place which he describes as lying "two hours' walk from here (about six miles), on fertile soil and near fine running springs."

LOCATION

Evidence points quite clearly to the hillside which ran back from the lot now occupied by the church and cemetery, as the place where they built their temporary shelters for the oncoming winter. There was a fine running spring at the foot of this hill, a delightful landmark still within the memory of persons now living, now disposed of through a drain from underneath one of the houses on the north side of East Herman Street.

On October twelfth, Pastorius received from the Frankford Land Company a warrant for 6,000 acres of land, and on the 24th he had the surveyor, Thomas Fairman, measure off fourteen (14) parcels of ground, one for each family, and one to be reserved for Pastorius himself. They are described in a letter by Herman op den Graeff as being 7 perches, or 115.5 feet wide, and deep enough to contain three acres of land. Pastorius says: "I laid out the town on October 24th and called it Germantown." The next day they met in his cave and drew lots for their several locations. The lot of the hillside and the spring and the temporary shelters was numbered four (4), and the one next to it, No.3, was assigned to Pastorius.

MEETINGS FOR WORSHIP

Here in their temporary houses, already in the process of construction, no doubt, when the lots were measured off, they at once began to hold meetings for united worship, though they had as yet no Minister among them. It was with this in view that Penn had directed their lots to be laid out so that they would "dwell together, that the children could be sent to school, and the neighbors could give each other a helping hand, and with united voices hold open prayer-meetings and sing their praises to the Lord." Thus it was that from this spot in the new settlement first ascended the sound of united praise and worship from German lips. The house occupied by Thones Kunders, who was the leader of the party, is generally spoken of as the place where these first meetings were held. Contrary to the usually accepted tradition, it must have been here, in his temporary house, and not in his later-built stone house fully a mile further down the road, that these first religious meetings were held.

Of either of these or similar meetings, Richard Townsend, a contemporary settler, writes: "Our first concern was to keep up and maintain our religious worship; and in order thereunto we had several meetings in the houses of the inhabitants . . . and having nothing but love and good will in our hearts one to another, we had very comfortable meetings from time to time; and after our meeting was over we assisted each other in building little houses for shelter."

DEATH AND BURIAL

A little over a month after their arrival on the spot, sorrow came to the little community through the death of one of their number. Herman op den Graeff wrote in a letter to the friends left behind: "My mother died on November nineteenth and was buried in this very place." Thus begins the history of this spot as a burying ground.

FIRST MEETING HOUSE

Being thus consecrated, this lot naturally became the place for the location of the first church in Germantown. Pastorius writes in one of his reports: "We have here in Germantown, in the year 1686, built a little church (*Kirchlein*) for the 'Gemeinde,' not with a view to an outwardly large stone structure, but that the temple of God (which we believers ourselves are) may be built up and all of us be nurtured in holiness and a godly life." That this was built primarily for and by the Mennonite settlers, and therefore on their ground, this statement leaves no room to doubt. Other suppositions, which have been advanced as to its location, lack substantiating evidence. We may assuredly assume, therefore, that this "Kirchlein" was the "little log meeting-house" which figures so largely in the early history of this place, and that it stood on the southwest corner of this lot, No.4, which afterwards, under the first survey, in the enlarged town, became lot No.19.

FIRST MINISTERS—ORGANIZATION

There was then no organized congregation as yet. They needed a Minister. Two years later, in the fall of 1688, Rev. William Rittenhouse came to Germantown from [Amsterdam], Holland, having probably been sent here to minister to the shepherdless flock. He, no doubt, at once began to exercise his ministry of the Word among them. Records show that lot No.19 was assigned to him in 1689. In [1698] an organization was formed by electing him as the regular Minister, with Jan Neues as Deacon. Rev. Dirck Keyser, who came the same year as Rittenhouse, was also recognized as a minister in the congregation, serving with Rittenhouse. In 1702 two more ministers were chosen, viz., Jacob Gaetschalk and Hans Neues, and Rittenhouse was ordained as the Bishop (Elder) of the congregation. Here, then, we see the beginning of the Mennonite Church in America.

On May 7, 1691, Thomas Lloyd, Deputy Governor, granted naturalization to sixty-two of the first inhabitants of Germantown, they, promising faith and allegiance to the King of Great Britain and the Proprietary, William Penn. The name of Francis Daniel Pastorius heads the list, which contains the names of at least fifteen Mennonites, including the two ministers, William Rittenhouse and Dirck Keyser.

In 1701, Rev. Rittenhouse conveyed the part of lot No.19 fronting on Main Street to Arnold van Fossen, who, in turn, February 10, 1702, conveyed that part on which the little log church stood, a lot 16.5 feet by 49.5, to John de Neues (John Nice) as trustee, on behalf of the Mennonites. Thus the little church came into the legal possession of the congregation.[2]

EARLY WEDDING

In this building two weddings were solemnized, of which records have been preserved. On April 6, 1692, Henry Frey, the carpenter, and Anna Catharine Levering were married by the Friends' ceremony before Francis Daniel Pastorius, thirty-two persons being present as witnesses. Among the signatures of these witnesses are found those of William Rittenhouse and Elizabeth Rittenhouse. The other wedding was that of Jacob Kolb and Sarah van [Sintern], on May 2, 1710, "in the presence of a full congregation in the little log meeting-house."[3] Rev. Dirck Keyser officiated. It is also thought that this building was used, for a time at least, for school purposes, with Pastorius as teacher.

SECOND BUILDING

By indenture dated September 6, 1714, Van Fossen conveyed a further part of this lot, containing 35 square perches, to Henry Sellen and John Neues, as trustees for the Mennonites, "for a place to erect a meetinghouse and a place to bury their dead," the deed distinctly restricting its use for the Mennonite church and cemetery forever. The growing congregation soon made use of this by erecting thereon a new building, presumably a frame structure, to take the place of the outgrown log church. It probably had two rooms, for church and school purposes respectively. Apparently the doors were on the side toward the cemetery and what is now Herman Street, a walk leading in from Main Street to the doors. The Rittenhouse Memorial Stone . . . stands on the space of this walk.

In this building Christopher Dock, "the pious schoolmaster of Skippack," taught school for some time. Two pieces of furniture used in his school, the teacher's table and one of the long seats, are preserved and still in use in the church. The table has the further distinction that on it was signed the first protest against slavery in this country, issued by these German settlers and addressed to the Friends' Meeting in 1688.[4]

PRESENT CHURCH

The building served the congregation a little over fifty years. In 1770, it gave way to the more durable stone building which stands at the same place and is still in a good state of preservation. . . . The rear part shown . . . was added in 1908, during the pastorate of Rev. J. W. Bayley.

A record of the cost of the building in 1770 was made by the carpenter, Mr. Jacob Knorr, whose personal bill for the carpenter work was £39 s12. He contributed £9 s10. The whole cost was £202 s5, which at the present rate of exchange [1923] would be a little less than $1,000. The records show further that some of the material of the old building was used.[5]

TIME BRINGS CHANGES

As for the congregation, it soon began to spread out into the fertile country sections to the north. Already in 1712, Rev. Gaetschalk, the then leading minister, in a report speaks of the Germantown congregation extending to the Skippack and numbering 99 members. But it was not long till the country settlements organized churches for themselves, and Germantown became the small end of the brotherhood. Then there came a time when there was no minister left here, and the services were supplied by ministers from the country congregations. By 1876 this support had become so intermittent and uncertain that the few members then connected with the church appealed to the Eastern District Conference for help and were taken under its wing, being admitted as a member of the Conference. From that time for a number of years the work at this place was under the oversight of the Pastor of the First Mennonite Church of Philadelphia, on Diamond Street; until in 1905 Rev. J. W. Bayley was chosen and ordained Pastor in full charge, and served faithfully until the time of his death, in March 1921. After the death of Rev. Bayley the congregation looked to the Home Mission Committee of the Eastern Conference for assistance. The present Pastor, Rev. A. S. Shelly, came in response to their united call, his pastorate dating from September 1921.

REORGANIZATION

When the present Deacon, Mr. Benjamin Bertolet, came to Rev. Bayley's assistance and identified himself with the work here, steps were at once taken to better organize the work. A set of rules and regulations was adopted, which had the effect of strengthening the activities of the church. In 1921 a movement to obtain a charter was set on foot. Through the kind and efficient direction of Maxwell H. Kratz, attorney-at-law, the application was made in due form and the charter was granted. Then an official survey of the premises was made, and a deed executed, approved and recorded, thus giving the new corporation legal title to the property. Mr. Bertolet also has made a study of the history of Germantown, with special attention to the Mennonite end of it. Out of the material he gathered, verified and supplemented by certain researches made by the present Pastor, the foregoing sketch has taken its shape.

Notes

1. This section is in part excerpted—with corrections where needed in the light of current research—from an informative 1923 "Historical Sketch," as found in the Appendix below.

2. That the little church was located on this property is being questioned by some current scholars.

3. The original indeed speaks of the wedding taking place "in unsser gemeinde in Germantaun," but does not state exactly the location. Whether or not it was in the little log meetinghouse cannot be ascertained.

4. Germantown Mennonite Church member Walter Temple, a human bridge between 1923 and the seventies, corroborated these details as to which table, and which long bench it was—the latter, in a taped interview with Melvin Gingerich in 1972. (I, Leonard Gross, remember vividly, around 1970/71, Temple's pointing to which table was the one upon which the 1688 petition had been signed and which bench was the original one, taken from the previous meetinghouse. See photos of the same, illustrated in this booklet.) Temple began attending the Germantown Church in 1919.

5. Some of these left-over materials from the old building are still extant, lying in the attic of the present Meetinghouse.

Select Bibliography

Many documents and volumes were consulted in the writing of this short history, most of which may be found in the Germantown Mennonite Historic Trust's research center. The sources listed below were found to be especially helpful.

Gleysteen, Jan, et al., Mennonite Church *Church Bulletin* series, 1983 (created at the occasion of the Germantown Tricentennial, 1683-1983).

Horst-Martz, Galen, "Restoring the Germantown Mennonite Meetinghouse: A Process," *Mennonite Quarterly Review*, 73 (April 1999), 303-05.

Miller, Joseph S. and Miller, Marcus, with Illustrations by Jan Gleysteen, *An Index and Description of The Mennonites of Southeastern Pennsylvania, 1683-1983.* Philadelphia, Pa.: Germantown Mennonite Church Corporation; Souderton, Pa.: Mennonite Historians of Eastern Pennsylvania, 1983.

Ruth, John L., *Maintaining the Right Fellowship.* Scottdale, Pa.: Herald Press, 1984.

_____. *'Twas Seeding Time: A Mennonite View of the American Revolution.* Scottdale, Pa.: Herald Press, 1976.

Smith, C. Henry, *The Mennonite Immigration to Pennsylvania in the Eighteenth Century.* Norristown, Pa.: Norristown Press, 1929.

Tinkcom, Margaret B., *Germantown and its Founders.* Germantown, Philadelphia, Pa.: Germantown Historical Society, 1983.

250th Anniversary of the Settlement of Germantown. Germantown, Philadelphia, Pa.: Germantown Historical Society, 1933.

The 240th Anniversary of the Coming of the First Mennonite Pilgrims and the Founding of Germantown. Germantown, Philadelphia, Pa.: Germantown Mennonite Church, 1923.

Wolf, Stephanie Grauman, *Urban Village: Population, Community, and Family Structure in Germantown, Pennsylvania, 1683-1800.* Princeton, N.J.: Princeton University Press, 1976.

See also scattered articles by Robert F. Ulle and others in the *Mennonite Quarterly Review, Pennsylvania Mennonite Heritage,* and the *Mennonite Historical Bulletin.*

An excellent popular booklet on the Mennonites and related groups, with selected bibliographical references, is the following: Kraybill, Donald B. *Who are the Anabaptists?—Amish, Brethren, Hutterites and Mennonite.* Scottdale, Pa.: Herald Press, 2003.

The Authors

Leonard gross, born in Doylestown, Pennsylvania, is a native of the Franconia Mennonite Conference in eastern Pennsylvania. He graduated from Goshen (Ind.) College in 1953. From 1955 to 1957 he worked with Mennonite youth throughout North Germany, an assignment with Mennonite Central Committee. He studied theology, ethics, and church history at the University of Chicago and the University of Hamburg, Germany. In 1959 he received the B.D. degree from Goshen Biblical Seminary and in 1968 (as a Fulbright Scholar, concentrating in church history, general history, and New Testament) the Ph.D. degree from the University of Basel, Switzerland.

From 1968 to 1970, Gross taught at Western Michigan University, Kalamazoo, Michigan. From 1970 to 1990 he served as Executive Secretary of the Historical Committee of the Mennonite Church, editor of *Mennonite Historical Bulletin*, and director of the Mennonite denominational archives and historical research program located at Goshen. He has written *The Golden Years of the Hutterites* (1980, rev. 1998). He translated and edited the classic (1708) *Prayer Book for Earnest Christians: a Spiritually Rich Anabaptist Resource* (1997). He edited and translated (with Elizabeth Bender) *Golden Apples in Silver Bowls: The Rediscovery of Redeeming Love* (1999)—a translation of a Swiss-Mennonite volume of early Anabaptist sources first published in 1702. He also co-authored *Selected Hutterian Documents in Translation, 1542-1654* (1975). His numerous articles on the Amish, Hutterites, and Mennonites have appeared over the decades in North American and European scholarly journals.

He and his wife, Irene (Geiser), live in Goshen, Indiana, and attend College Mennonite Church. They are the parents of two grown daughters, Suzanne and Valerie. Gross currently serves on the executive of the Mennonite Historical Society.

As a child in the 1930s, Gross remembers, he experienced profound awe each time his father purposefully drove past the old stone Mennonite Meetinghouse on Germantown Avenue. He has been a board member of the Germantown Mennonite Historic Trust since 1970, helping to preserve this same Colonial Germantown Mennonite Meetinghouse built in 1770.

JAN GLEYSTEEN was born and raised in Amsterdam, Holland, the oldest child of Mennonite bookseller Jan Gleysteen and his wife, Gerritje. As a young adult he studied illustration and design at the Municipal School of Fine Arts and at the Royal Academy. During the early 1950s he crisscrossed Europe on his bike, sketching and painting along the way, including the places from where the original Germantown families emigrated.

Gleysteen came to the United States in the fall of 1953 to study at Goshen (Ind.) College and to start his work at the

Mennonite Publishing House, Scottdale, Pennsylvania. He served the church close to forty years as artist, writer, editor, and traveling lecturer. In 1969 Gleysteen teamed with Mennonite writer and filmmaker John L. Ruth on the first of many research trips to document, pictorially, Anabaptist-Mennonite history, life, and thought. Two of Gleysteen's published works are: *The Drama of the Martyrs* (1975) and *Mennonite Tourguide to Western Europe* (1984).

Gleysteen's interest in Germantown was kindled by historian J. C. Wenger in the late 1950s; and the Germantown story has continued to fascinate him ever since. For the Germantown Mennonite Tricentennial, 1683-1983, Gleysteen created a series of four pen-and-ink illustrations, plus texts telling the Germantown story. These resources still are widely used in books and periodicals.

Now retired in Goshen, Indiana, Gleysteen continues to speak and lead tours. He and his wife Barbara are members of College Mennonite Church. They are the parents of two grown children, Linda Gleysteen and David Gleysteen. Jan Gleysteen also is a board member of the Germantown Mennonite Historic Trust.

GROSS took the lead in the writing of the text, and GLEYSTEEN in creating the visuals and the map. The two worked hand in hand, attempting to bring a unity and wholeness to each of the parts.

Photo Credits: The photographs in Part II are from the Heritage Keeper collection of Jan Gleysteen, except for the photos of the Mennonite Meetinghouse and the slavery protest table (p. 43), and the bench (p. 44), which were supplied by Randy Nyce. Grateful acknowledgment is made for permissions granted by Elizabeth Ryder for use of *The Landing of William Penn*, 1682, by J. L. G. Ferris (p. 33); and to the Delaware Art Museum for the use of *The Attack upon the Chew House* (also known as *The Battle of Germantown*), by Howard Pyle (p. 45). The six linedrawings scattered through the book are of unknown origin but were used repeatedly in Germantown programs, brochures, and publications during the late nineteenth and early twentieth centuries.